THE
PHARMACY

KAT SINCLAIR

Published 2024 by the87press
The 87 Press LTD
87 Stonecot Hill
Sutton
Surrey
SM3 9HJ
www.the87press.co.uk

The Pharmacy © Kat Sinclair, 2024

The moral right of Joseph Coward has been asserted in accordance with the Copyright, Designs and Patents Act 1988

ISBN: 978-1-7393939-9-1

Printed and bound by CPI Group (UK) Ltd, Croydon, CR0 4YY

Design: Stanislava Stoilova [www.sdesign.graphics]

for Dad
for Jess

'The line between poison and medicine is subtle.'
—Umberto Eco, *The Name of the Rose*

'The *pharmakon*. . .is neither speech nor writing'
—Jacques Derrida

'hope how do I confess when pain has taken up every language available'
—Cat Chong, *Dear Lettera 32*

Part I—Eulogy
*

The Pharmacy
The General
Death Rattle
Lament
Second Fit
*

Rise Again
Last Words
My Metonym
Objets Da

Part II—Lament
*

RSH
New Review
Watching
Mineral Miracle Solution
Once Again
Spectacle
Sorry I Can't I'm Slammed
Last Poem
New Build
Another England Poem
*

Getting The Measure
To Roam
Prescription

Absolute State Of It
Not Sure Yet
Liberal Demo
*

Old Steine
Diptych
Royston Smith MP
Extrapolate

Part III—Elegy
*

Outlet
Tuesday
In Public
Return
Child Poem
Tired
*

Words Mean Things?
More Of That
Repatriation
Lining
State Care
Ad Asteracaeae
Smear
Unaccounted For In The Studies
*

I Am Well
Dead Skin

Two Factor
Kitchen Table
Sorry
Airing Cupboard
Particulier
Dissolve
Pathologic Hypertrophy

Part IV—Reverie
Later
Resignation From

Part I—Eulogy

*

A means of producing
extra cells,
how generous.

A logic of growth
we cannot
pick and choose.

More is more
we say
so we say more again.

The Pharmacy

Part and parcel
old building rust
maze
incomprehensibility of layout
reflective

Ponder tendons
and which part of the state do they resemble?
This remains Burke's organic society
everything in its place our
brain the patriarch of the rest
in that prison of the torso

Disappear distinction dissolve
when experiencing physical deterioration as
something happening outside the mind
/ you can't be helped, that is a kind of death
—palliative care for the dualist

We are all about life extension man
who wants to extend his life—
we know this about him, and nothing else

> *There is a big hole in your head*
> *I can see it on a screen*
> *Therefore,*

One doubts
things happening inside the body
a conspiracy of the self that is not yours
while the doctor-doubt

refracts and you dismiss
poor air quality
environmental racism
or your trailing somewhat guts

I am the only imperfect rememberer I can accept
I call myself to court
I listen to my tales
I demand
a royal fucking story
a star power witness
I take the stand

> *In books, when people look into each other's eyes, they are reminded of a pool they swam in in childhood, or some mysterious forest from a National Geographic, or an oil slick they stepped in and cried. This has never happened to me.*

Smells like cedarwood and masculinity
I don't have a nose for that kind of sentiment
though I try
wine, perfume, scent-training night school—
there is no unskilled labour!
even this jogging of the memory takes work
so give it a whiff:

Generalise: smell good, smell familiar
smell sick, smell dead.
Yet, old Superdry perfume,
rests crystalline, empty, and specific
on my windowsill

Focus the beach body politic
of work

of water
in parts
the word 'care' singed on our thigh
in the absence of suncream

Lovely little liberals
our language of medicine
is a language of poison
but those blue lights call me in
like a church on a hill,
I have been climbing for hours and the light
flickers

> *Cat called it a 'loveless lexicon'*
> *this cytotoxic substance*
> *like nostalgia,*
> *fascism is necessarily rose-tinted*

Regardless, reading the words
'The NHS is an enemy of Britain'
twists and lodges,
we cannot critique, like this
we cannot make you better

Conspiracy theory into conspiracy praxis—
write that in your magazine and smoke it

Ultimately I exist only in that space of twenty minutes
between a district nurse who could not choke the word
palliative,
'take your pills'
man without a mouth
cruel healing stab
and you, who asked me knowingly

to decide if a fluffed-pillow jostle
'we can turn him?'
soft killing blow
we who understand that
logic of the almost-end
thinning 'thank you' veil

The pharmacy cannot fulfil.

The General

Bus goes by,
imagining if you could plagiarise equations
"I did that one"
or sue somebody for getting the same disease.

Slippage like language
the more similar the closer the more obvious the gaps
squeaking, crackling, polystyrene inverted, the white space,
grief is *like this*
sickness is *like this*:
the closer you come to me the starker our worsenings.
I need a support group consisting entirely of people
who have had the polar opposite
of the same experience as me and only then
will I feel held—
it is not a competition, but I find myself astride the horse's back
galloping, all the same.

They took the fast food chain out of the hospital foyer
last meal triple cheeseburger and two boxes of fries
no matter what has to be fished out
later, for now all is delicious
all must be.

This time the son devouring Saturn
we should cry 'justice' but we wince collective,
his stomach distended, he can't hack it,
instead we turn our backs though it is good to witness failure
it is failure to identify.

While she's

checking for lumps
in my yoghurt.

Summer's roar it is an affront
to make it stagnant in verse
I have to move the language on
not pull the action back to meet me
but I can't,
my hands still shake from the holding and
I cannot form a fist.

thinking through the fuck-it to a
future like trying to imagine how
the offspring of a small dog and a big dog came to be
with the puppy in your lap, crying for attention—
but who was the male dog—
evidence of the now gets bored, hop-leaping away

catheter on my old childhood clothes hanger

new definitions of clean.

Death Rattle

It's more than you can bear,
every 'met this lovely gentlemen' a thieves' cant,
but the pharmacist tells you to
bang on the door—they're in there, curdling and private
while you ossify.

You were pedantic until the very end and
it may have been more poetic to lie, like
'the internalised instruments of class,
language of Imperial civility, well they fall
away in the face of the great don't-believe-in-it-
but-still-it-snarls-in-potentiality' instead
your grammar perfect until the awful silent choke,
hands and eyes, you legislate.

Lament

Devotionals
in the way I wince before
eating a fairground doughnut,
I will never ride the waltzers now
those teacups ate at Nan's leg, grinding metal,
leaping muscle-memory 'cross the spin
and *still*, not much more to say.
Especially to you, now you can't hear—
and thank God for that, it was the last thing to go
you heard my light mock
I knew you found it funny, 'just grabbing a tea and
YOU CAN'T HAVE ONE'
but what if you didn't?
Hindsight gets murky, actually.

Second Fit

Triage
Outpatient
Corridor
Your broken back on wheels

> *The moon is a puzzle to solve*
> *flushed and sweating, hugged and loosening*

the vessels of the city are inaccessible
blockages en route
signifying nothing, really, but of great cruel inconvenience
to be floating around in there,
while the charred lungs balloon and deflate
you want to pop them, mobility aid spiking
'Let's meet up, it's been so long, I'm only 10 mins on the tube.'

there was, I saw, a death canal, all
barge, dam, lock, narrow
levels adapting to our passing
pumping calm the system
great feat of engineering
Charon's crossing must be like this:
slow, straight, carved like bone

that video of the rescue beaver:
instinctive stuffed blockage,
a barricade of cuddly toys, dragged and dumped
there is an unnatural nature of the good—
a care and raising of flat tail to hardwood floor,
dragging a miniature Christmas tree,
knowing he is at home, despite it, even so—

it is like loving you still,
to drag things to the threshold, prevent the flood,
see nothing will flow through and I have made a mess
but I have done my duty,
beavering intuition,
drag another, needless: plug the gap.

> *Love doesn't die it goes to sleep*
> *I coax it, morning tea, wake up soft so*
> *feel the beachy streams run through, salt over loss*
> *wake up or dry up, that never-numb itch.*

My ablutions are as follows:
Stop! Rendering the neutral masculine in retrospect!
Stop! Retroactively rendering the neutral masculine!
'What do men have that feels like
[image of 100000 beauty products]?'
Beer, sports, LEGO, music.
Tech makes everything difficult for Mum.

On the ward so long you're a disgruntled local
tutting the newcomer, surveyor,
part of the infrastructure: rusting and staid.

Still hoping to write that campus novel,
so I'm still on campus,
holding the funeral gift: Diana Funko POP

I want to live so far away from the ambulance dispatch centre
forgetting that exact shade of intermittent blue
fade interminably, intolerably on
now I can process:
dog on hunger strike
everyone getting Lasik

shoulder locking again

The focus group rises up, singing
songs from another advert
tearing down the proposed campaign slogans
not even saving the feedback form
for blackout poetry, there is nothing to be salvaged
in Meeting Room A, this palace of the sick,
synecdoche calling security,
take them down, they've lost focus.

It's so retro now: Coughs and sneezes spread diseases!
Rhyme passé, we've moved onto greener pastures,
rule of three, podium proud,
rock, paper, die.
A frantic poetic cadence, I am jealous of the slowdown, I can't effect it.

Welcome to the reading, here's your plebiscite:

> *I love this city*
> *everyone hates.*

Crackling reception, cheap little dress,
taking too long with the catheter can't she see
there's a queue,
husk yourself, move along, let not water pass your lips
but smile, and smile.

Rather like: requesting one too many scans and triggering the endgame
the body does not like being looked at,
punishment for checking,
here goes.

Abolish the family history
send me out and set me down,
mittens and winter salad,
I know not what lurks,
nor what burst through and out
my doctor, not a cunt, for once:
we have no information
on which to base a 'you should—'
see, this is bliss
see, this is morning again
with a headache and a text message.

> *The shipping forecast hisses, in my grandfather's voice:*
> *there'll be ships.*

Still, I think the units of harm
set out on suburb lawns-in-competition
collect their dues and I long for
that rudderless drift,
which is not abolitionism,
for I have replaced nothing—no winter salad,
no mittens, no friends at the table,
but whatever works to empty my head
of my mind, of my brain and all its signals.

*

At some point we have to admit it's just not working.

No we don't.

Rise Again

By the sink, 'this dying thing is boring'
like a video game Easter Egg
I found out you were quoting:
proof of life after death,
two-factor authenticated.

Exporting to .zip, digital coffin
stay there until I dig you up
rob our conversational grave when I need the gold teeth,
the real idiomatic gems
get stuck in my throat forever, I won't swallow because I can't.

> *Scared that you'll forget me*
> *have never known me*
> *an ancient baby a brand new man.*

Domestic medical equipment,
catheter hooked, dangling from a clotheshanger
so I think about abortion.

> *I don't want to give you your last cup of tea.*

Thames Gardens
Did it hurt when she died?
What shape was the scar?

Memory Dad and Allison
dead glass hand scars door—
Dad's first wife doesn't know he's dead.

Myelin sheath is a border too

and these neat borders between family members
Drowning in Aunt-Death
3/5 siblings down.

> *Pacman ghosting in the shop*
> *aisles of don't notice me yet*
> *I am here I am*

emerging—
young and not yet ready to be made older
in relative relational relativity
when you look at me I am a *visitor*.

Last Words

I'll be nil by mouth when I die
so load me up beforehand
with all my favourite everything
choking

quietly beatify:
act of swabbing,
artificial saliva,
Kiwi and Lime, lovingly

in the home

no uniform change:
the slyness of the body
its incoherent waning
slack pull of skin over bone
turned steroidal puff
waxy feel, tender cup and stroke
nothing so loving as the cheek

streetlight, tarmac, tile

run headlong into it, wire fence
nearly an A road
it was your prerogative and
I tried to keep it so

shrill fox fuck

trundle
habitual

biding
glean

I think we let George Osborne off the hook
by the way,
goodbye now.

My Metonym

It has been three years and I am still learning bridge by osmosis
my subscription box ghosts
are all my fathers and I touch their cheeks,
press too hard and the flickering.

The illusion of the private is dissolved
by the influencer and the cancer patient both
so that it feels familiar, this utter everywhereness:
everywhere a hospital, everywhere a pharmacy,

Everywhere the potential for wilful discharge
against advice, don't you dare say the death word—
even at home you are not at home
even in my arms you are somewhere else.

'A mask or mould made before you start treatment—
 they can also be called shells.'
I see mesh now where there was total plastic,
this damnable progress.

My beloved reminder that others should be grateful for what
they have a nodal concern on the NHS app
an oddbox, a misstep, an accessible fucking teacup.
You put your left arm in.

Objets Da

How can you possibly know
what you'll wish you'd taken down to the bunker
after you close the door?

Justify with 'he would want you to', and he wouldn't, and
that kitchen cupboard was cytotoxic, and now
it is full of dog treats,
no repentance necessary. It's time for walkies.

He was: launching a formal complaint because
they were playing the Macarena
in the radiotherapy machine.
I was: mining the document for material.

Found this: that when the fracture clinic signed him off,
he got a little taller with the healing
and the Strongbow advert screeched its merry way towards
us, saccharine as the product itself and half as fizzy

Can't go scrumping, it's lockdown.
But I don't think they know what scrumping is to ban it
I could—
pretend I'm out shooting grouse
with twenty-nine of my closest friends
or risk it all for a non-essential apple, alone.

On the back porch and maybe out-living you but
better than nothing, which is anything.

While it's brewing: a radiotherapy mask
at the bottom of the stairs.

It has a bracket on it with screws which fixed him to the table.
It looks like it's perpetually screaming.
It has his name on it.

This is normal. This is one of the most normal things there is.
That, in itself, is unbelievable. My personal window
an overturned louse
caught in the gaps on the sole of my shoe.
Where I store the rest of it, questions like:
"Where are my baby videos?"
Requests like: "Don't say 'remission.' It hurts me."

The algorithms change
on the shared accounts.

Together in electric dreams.

Part II—Lament

*

Will of the people:
we leave it all to us.

RSH

Car park interminable
render in-the-know, ticket tricks
if you're lucky enough to be always
in appointments, slip out under the
old psychiatric building, still in use
after a quick Google, reversing,
you literally cannot tell from the outside.

When I am walking back from the job centre
through absence-of-tram,
once ducking thrill, I sketch my own near-decapitation
if only we hadn't been bombed—
nevermind, flanked by lions either side,
restored to former glory, foreskin pulled slightly back
this golden garish day!

Easy division, don't get too used to it:
he will knit you together in the wombing
Solent tide, freeport establish,
once more at the match and smiling—
this is a good idea, why can't we just get along?
East-West divide, unaccountable,
surmountable, scum—
he's scored an absolute worldie, he'll say,
and how fitting, from Mayflower Park.

Here is where it starts out:
wide hat tilt, Rose out the car,
they say she's unsinkable—
Or, here is where it ends up:
couldn't hack it in the communitarian land of Surrey

(it is a kick in the teeth, to visit the mounds,
a track alongside, a whistling ghost of Empirical rush,
next to the bold attempts)
so, down to the docks and off, off out, out there
we won't have to think about it again.

This place has been,
and over there it was:
fishhook of post-industry to the gut,
this reclaimed land, dredged from that wet bastard—
lapping right up against the once-wall,
I am standing on the bridge and straddling the border
with great grimace,
weight shifting, on so much funicular exostosis,
most marginal door, the fridge light flickering
while the vegetables sweat.

Cleave to the sight of the boats on the spit
like the old psychiatric building, but in ungoogleable relief—
Are we in use? Returning results by so many
medicated SEO content specialists,
full circle moment, blue sky thought: yes.

New Review

Knowing we're in a 'bad' 'place' because
the poetry is starting to resemble the politics
wherein everything is just a list of things you want
to happen to another person like

> *'I hope your glasses are never clean*
> *I hope the vending machine always gets stuck*
> *I hope your vibrator runs out of battery*
> *I hope you can't get comfy'*

I bet you fucking liked that didn't you
Very Skittish Problems we're afraid to identify
the source or to accost it for real
in the corridors of power we like the plush carpet

Appreciate the natural light
cutting your cheek at a particular angle
take satisfaction in the fact—well,
what are you waiting for?

My unlimited conversational repertoire has found
its limit in this: inability to recognise the heart of the other,
only the sound, and words can be fresh
while the inside politely rots

I hope we rip it out.

Watching

All of this raising
questions of self-indulgence a
Brave Man Standing Up Meme
declares 'It is morally acceptable to write
about yourself.' There are few things
less necessary than
this gloaming confessional
skirting violence, like this one.

What can a poem do? *More than this*
hundred thousand spread
in record time, with record receipt
cawing capture:
this is what it is like
to be a Millennial
watching a genocide
in real time.

If that does indeed answer a question
some way down the line
we spit at he who asks it
all eyes elsewhere
where gloaming calls violence
amid no hospital lights
no brave Western soul-search
no confession without witness.

Mineral Miracle Solution

Strong belief, bowing in high city wind,
whistling: a poetics of whatever's going on
with the conspiracy theorists,
inclined to demand it.

Gleeful state broadcaster
segment an introduction to
giving Ivermectin more air
time was, airborne disease moved
faster than this, but everyone caught up:
drink it down, anti-parasitic,
all that information, clinically meaningful.

Until rostering clumsily forwards
autistic-adjacent-family-desperate-crazy-bright:
this rodeo so familiar it flickers blue to purple,
clicked, fire-hot and roll-eyed,
I introduce the mommies to my dearest friends
wondering what else, beyond bleach,
creeping undersea, presenting: a cure.

Imported American dialectical Empire
in concert with real-time: a circus,
with bear-baiting
such that this, interminable termite, burrowing
a maze, single-pixel-wide,
through sense, a hyperbaric echo-chamber
(for horses!)
meanwhile the whole of us gerrymandered
through the great unreasonable adjustment
denied.

While I Dungeon Synth my way through
another bout of RSI you
contradict, you clown college scholarship, you
superpositional state of existence (bleach)
and nonexistence (go outside),
you vape.

There are only so many times
one can touch grass before
all blades are crushed underhand.

Still, keep a magnifying eye:
tiny grass is dreaming.

Once Again

Bernadette I try to change the language but he gets there first:
sad! Grammar of the cairn,
I need not know what's inside,
only what is stacked around it,
that someone did the stacking on their way.

Experimental writing project
too on the nose too much salad too much retrograde
too much workplace too much campus too much transit
repetition, I have seen it all
and I have seen it in New York.

But wake to lover's Sharpie on an upper thigh
scrawled: speak to repeated discourse without explicitly
repeating it on my right breast: what is SUBTLETY
on my left breast: what is DIDACTICISM
an advertisement for Peta's literary branch.

Strike up the brass band march for the
mass datafication of reviewing
but I cannot write through
as I am supposed to
we have created a one poetics of pain.

Spectacle

Saw Napoleon's death mask at a goth cocktail bar
in London and thought of Benjamin,
thought of how much I love
repetitive lines that change meaning
over the course of a piece of writing,
thought of Adania Shibli,
thought the prize is the death mask of the work
yet, still: I rage.

Told a joke at the publisher party and it goes like:
tyranny of the majority!

Learn that music is not a thing it's an absence,
think that spectacle is dead.

I figured it out:
isopod
at the bottom of the ocean
with a packet of crisps.

When the submarine exploded
all-the-way-down-there
death of the moment, end of history again
can't crane our heads,
Cronenbergian *Crash*,
to look at the disaster.

A cat eating a tiny world.

Sorry I Can't I'm Slammed

We saw her, gifting her one year old
a set of building blocks:
a hierarchy of needs—
chubby hand comes DOWN
on the pyramid and there's a BREAK in the lounge system—
we start again, bird nest tireless.

The new horizon of justice is to be located
in the Hot Tub Showroom
next to the Fareham Kebab stand
where we set them all going at once
until the jury's so bubbly-relaxed we just
can't stand it anymore.

These are: actionable objectives—
or they would have been in the Summer of '76, like most things
you have a choice: write happy songs or face full of mud
you cannot do both, caked in it, mouth full of worm
harmonies, don't be petulant:
the shotgun marriage of sadness and self-worth.

"It is okay to have a brand name,"
we reassure our clients. They will hate you for it,
but you will be amenable to a merger,
and that's worth ten of them. Chin up, love.
They're just jealous of your efficiency—
this is how they show it.

Last Poem

Another defection walk across the aisle
dredges up another scandal from newspapers' past
'you couldn't write it' but you did—
any more of this and we'll be out there on our doorsteps,
those of us with doorsteps, clapping for the IEA.

> *This House believes*
> *it was rendered narrow to elevate levels of stress*
> *a Haussmannisation in reverse*
> *their barricades, acceptable*
> *ours, no longer bridging the gap.*

Another scroll, another tweet, screams 'the experience
of scrolling past bloodied corpses sandwiched between
a Negroni and a weight loss ad' sandwiched between
another tweet screaming the experience and
another poetics of the Internet, here.

> *This House believes*
> *in nothing if it cannot be delivered by quango,*
> *shovelled down the throat only just sicked,*
> *we are helpless in the nest,*
> *we are scientifically managed, one branch per bird.*

Knowledge in snippets,
a magazine ransom note of a world-
view— breakage, representational
but choke up through from the under-language say
fire.

New Build

I have become enamoured of local history
in place of where I could've gone the other way
(plant identification,
the Linnaean wrong kind)
but while you can take the anthropocentrism
out of the girl...! You can't.
It is good to know what buildings used to be
when there are buildings.
But learning Liverpool St. Station was once an asylum
there are *sites* and there are bombed-out
sinkholes of semi-recorded memory
What was that? Was it anything?
I am certain people suffered there
even before the explosion.
I assume this is Coventry, too,
some husk-growth in the soul
so that visitors will crow at the great
nothing-except-a-hopping-centre
when there was a castle there, once,
and isn't that beautiful and worse?
Unsinkable ship, map on the floor of the museum, red dots
those we know. What else? So much constellation
it ceases to be so and becomes instead, the sky.
All this to say the hospital was once an infirmary
for the inmates of Southampton workhouse,
but it was elsewhere and the site on which it is built—
They are connecting up our two cities,
slowly, a *Creation of Adam*
in new-build grey and it is only a matter of time
before they cover the field on which your ashes danced.

Another England Poem

This place, every day
a dry roast dinner of the soul

This poorhouse to hospital to theatre
royal-destroyed by a fire in 1884—
it's flats now
Jane Austen Visited Here
and who else?

> *Looked round at a dog too fast,*
> *whipped neck,*
> *sweaty paws,*
> *swept ink,*
> *sally forth!*

Disinfecting the rental car
farewell to James
it has been four years of it

Our place
rude snatching jagged ends
pick it up and smoke it and there's still something there
past the crush, under-heel

> *A Mick Lynch poem:*
> *isn't there suddenly a strike?*
> *I believe in a thing called out,*
> *capturing the texture of the time*
> *sex like nouning a verb*
> *notre dame de brûler*

Stuff undeniable despair,
factor three she woke up tracked and breezed

and blitzed and wheezed down the hall and sank,
skirt rucking

Into the breakfast bar:
what kind of person is still shaped by the academic
wheel of the year at thirty?

May the shellfish be fresh and may we all be close to the sea,
as close as we will it.

*

The woman at the bus stop tells me she was determined to make it to her appointment this morning despite the fact her daughter is working and so she has to take her grandson along and there he is in his buggy hi hello and she has to get two buses across town and was nearly late and she very nearly missed it and I, waiting for the same bus (I to work, her to home), which is late, am sorry she is having such an exhausting day and she says thank you did you know there were *two missed appointments* before she went in and it is shameful and it is the reason our NHS is in the state it is in and I wonder how they are their daughters and their sickness and their buses on their side of town, and how late they are, and our is a productive word and a shroud and a bezoar.

Getting The Measure

For illegal dismissal of

Boycotting the

Buying it up and burning it

If their idea of salient critique is calling everything a 'brigade'

what can we learn?

> *A Jeremy Corbyn of the right*
> *A comedy of the right*
> *A lackadaisical spirit of the right*
> *A breakfast of the right*
> *A camera obscura of the right*
> *A water-based lube of the right*
> *A scented candle of the right*
> *A Taskmaster of the right*
> *A noise cancelling headphones of the right*
> *A giant African land snail of the right*
> *A molasses of the right*
> *A washing line of the right*
> *A flapjack of the right*
> *A Miracle Gro of the right*
> *A prenup of the right*
> *A repetitive strain injury of the right*
> *A nihilism of the right*
> *A world of the right*

too busy at circus school
to learn better communication—
HONK!

How can we learn from the right?

> *How can we learn from the right?*

'They're using memes' was always a bit tired
but I forgave you, Dark Fruits in hand,
spine on standby,
thinking surely he's got something better than that
but by Summer I was gone and I never found out, lolz.

Nihil est a contradiction in terms
'stop caring' less a kek flag than a white one,
ironies abound. It is good to be anonymous
only in these circumstances,
but I want to be known to you, less celebrity more
hold me when I cry, and when you do
let me be more than a username.

Dockside dangling, come on in, the water's shit
but we are once again tracking freighters
discussing weapon degradation in RPGs in light of Barthes'
Reality Effect—we are so, so into reality

that pitter-patter of tiny barges
in the strait,
we're so proud,
we've named her Gillian,
she contributes less than 3%
to transport-based carbon emissions per annum.

If you were balding I would love you more,
vulnerable pate,
is that a problem? Probably.
I am suspicious of your upper lip,

moustache elegantly able to smuggle a sneer
undetected, past my little jokes,
do you even lick your upper lip?
If not, do you miss it?
Could you mark how much you miss it on a scale of one to ten?
Could you be objective, please?
Is that all?
Well we'll have to see about other options, then.
Perhaps we'll reassess come Springtime.
Here's your script,
I've said my lines now
you say yours

and swallow. Good.
Now try shaving, nice and smooth,
as close as you can.

To Roam

Told me to go out and enjoy nature
go home Google 'what is "nature"'
scroll peach hue little bit of lip another racist overlay
for an image sodden with *today*
finally informed there is such a thing as 'walks'
lest I give up, go be unnatural in the bath

it's unfortunate that I have to look up
and see nothing at all,
otherwise we'd never have camped out
at the planning meeting, unfortunate
but essential, we hit our quota for
dreaming spires, centuries ago.

Knowing the difference in degrees
I take it upon myself,
pressing the thermometer to the lawn
to each lawn in each personal garden
and shaking my head, wondering
if a personal Eden requires a personal pesticide

but we divvied up the arable land,
prettier now,
absolutely barren,
but that patchwork sight on landing
is worth it, all those shades of fucking
useless green, see me through.

Prescription

Fascist state practices through medicine
in plenitude

Give the housewives back their barbiturates
please the baby is crying

Always reading the word subduing in conjunction
with 'ADHD' – is this antirevolutionary medicine?!

Doctors overwhelmed by the volume
of work 'it feels like a checkout'

As does the biopolitical countdown
how many times have I flushed the toilet today?

The Deserving Poor never died, not really
so we still foot the bill

The public purse
a household debt of the Kingdom

If only they hadn't insisted on metaphor in debate
we'd have fewer threads from economists

Cure and its exact opposite
can mean either inside or outside

Speech or writing
a scapegoat

Those 'on benefits'
a means of producing a narrative

> *'In this way writing reveals another writing,*
> *masked by its derived or common meaning.'*

The factory is a pharmakon
or the hospital is a factory

Producing diagnosis
he only had it, official, after that appointment

Producing that diamond-rare
'shared care'

Something can be healing and destructive,
I suppose

Psychiatry, you tell me
'I am dying of a long word.'

Faking illness to treat the cause
instead magnetising oneself, iatrogenic

Insurance covers the wheelchair
not the app to drive it

> *'Writing is a pharmakon in a composite sense of*
> *these meanings as "a means of producing something".'*

They cut the trees down and blocked off the car park
so we can no longer access the nothing

Using my not-keys to enter my not-house
if I am not out of the requisite battery to do so

Honour the world translucent, plastic, causing

frantic concern for the tardigrade

Back to the viaduct, mise-en-abyme-en-Hayward's-Heath
(the hospital there, impossible)

Needlework and translation pain
consent form, health and wealth

A kinder gentler technostate
sends all the politicians to a chicken pox party

Fentanyl is good for some things
but I wish it killed cops too.

Absolute State Of It

No man is on an island, not anymore
o' crumbling school
o' Wilko's last vestige
don't you worry, you can still buy the pick n mix
through the online store:
bricks and mortar
shepherd's crowning
rising water
shepherd's drowning
frantically swiping 'life hacks for surviving the relentless rise' and
finding relief in the inevitability of it:
of course, a clothes hanger!
I need that vocal fry in a drip,
my kidneys are *sound*, no, literally.

that summer we got jealous of their whole
saving the children thing
an alloy of correct suspicion and wrong conclusion
my microplastics practically glowing with pleasure
interrupt the treatment plan: start again with the right
    attitude this time

Last night I had a dream I was in
a controlling relationship with Elon Musk
Mark Ruffalo was trying like Hell to get me out of there
but I could not make it out,
the writing on the wall: now what?

beauty and kindness in
buying a hairless cat and knitting it a jumper

oh the department is *Christian*
like some sort of medical Veggietales
you say it's good for me,
chaplain in the waiting room
I am sixteen days into goodbye and here to get
my medication, but you are installed here, somehow
prompting an almost-outrage
IS THIS BUILDING NOT THE STATE
before I remember we don't have that here, nominal—
you are intrinsic, entitled to, encouraged and
paid.

Everything is someone's job but
nothing is happening.

Did Stanisława Przybyszewska die
of Robespierre or do we simplify the real
collapse the political and as the sausage is made
mad women are piped in, filling out, delicious
in her letters she is furious, Wittigian,
but we love a pining dog at the train station of history
when the professor has been dead for years
mistaking emotion for impotence,
fervour for fiction—
in the last nights of Ventôse never-ended.
Fill out the form until the dodgy internet cuts out
and erases everything
do *not* go again,
this is the correct amount of nothing.

Not Sure Yet

In love we are,
tangled like a pair of IUD strings

tugging,
an epidemic of not getting it out

experimental poetry tiny boxes zoom,
the life cycle of the poetic imaginary

pushing at the inner corner of each eye to check
my blind spots are still there

clam shell phone case
using the word 'gauche'

watching an act of self immolation
where your only response is 'ouch'

can of worms
nuke the family the silent treatment

you were supposed to outlive your sisters
I want to recommend you books forever

what would it be to write confessional poetry
other than an exercise in fanfiction for the soul

blushing and bowing and nominated
a whole season has been dropped at once and I am

glutting on the produce
the woman games a book

the carrots are purple and we smile
knowingly, and when we purple do they share the same

how to talk about this
worries: boring, distressing, excessive

reading about the eighteen year old girl
on the subway with the scarf

everybody is always already dead,
it's like I'm paid to think it!

Liberal Demo

I am supposedly doing some imaginative work
requiring a certain amount of focus
Like—'what would be your job on the centrist commune?'
A person deserving of a 'roster' would stick to the concept
and step two: profit, it's like a dating app but you're
pictured with your arms around your best critical lenses
But I am slippery all over the places writing on a triangulation
from I have exes in all three of these cities and you could
localise me, right there, on that suburban lawn wearing
nothing but an undone thing
pushed to the side so you can see
I have nothing to hide, not now it's gone away

The guy vested with the power to Fund taps the sign it says
stick to the point or circle it like a ravenous stuck hyena but
instead I sick up something like
There are two things certain in this life death and praxis
death and faxes death and anaphylaxis
I am ejected from the premises but told to come back when
I get a better handle on Form so that I might upset it more
intentionally

It was a beautiful day in the close to the boundary line blue
heartland pumping in a sea of red when we the children
and I split the traffic in the road and sat so they might learn
the difference between good disruptions and bad ones and
I reached out and pulled up a weed growing through the
cracks because I have an undiagnosed disorder of great
limbed structure and the weed caught the eye of a child and
screamed

'Forgive me father for I have sinned I have failed to build a
profitable business after raising a substantial amount of funds
under the claim of innovation and disruption I am a $699
juicer and I have been beaten to a pulp by the market at last'

This is a way of connecting what must be connected via what
already is
Pulling the lever to switch the tracks
Like weaving or gerrymandering
The natural world in total opposition to my breakfast bowl
of chrome and glass as if there were never any sand

When I texted him last night
I am sick
But don't worry, this isn't IT
He thought I meant IT like 'IT' when I just meant it like 'it'
But this has been a couple years of conflations at a stark rate
of increase
So I can be forgiven even if IT can't, or the other one

I suppose my role on the centrist commune would be just that
The indecipherability of this one and that one,
adding a drop more mud to the water and giving it a
delicate, unpartisan stir
only a certain amount of inbetweenness concentrated in the
ginfusion but just enough to give you a funny little feeling in
your mouth—ooh!
I would suck them, NOT crunch them,
then one of the commune party leaders takes another yellow
look at me and I hear the projected result:
"Going out dressed like that? On a JUBILEE year?"

This is all the imaginative work I am capable of between des

petites collapses—
like death but you have to get up again, go to work, put the pen down,
somebody made another joke about the insect thing but
the absurd has fallen straight through the trap of its own
arsehole so that it's stranger now
to wake up human, and answer questions.

*

If you don't know anything
it's cool: the dragon, the sword

Keynesian rotting, can be proud of the plug socket

I like the look of that new kit flag. Shame.

Old Steine

Joined you down by the
campaigning for destability rights activism
slathering my skin with unfinished projects
then checking the pH: it's a number, and isn't it always
incapable of describing anything in monodirectional phrase
you ask how I am and I say:
when you sit down wrong
on a desperate night
and get piss on your skirt.

We Calvinist queers think we're the good half of it
like, saved by a Jesus Dyke for President
but our preterition seeps through
like all desperate liquids do and
we find ourselves not, raised up
instead: voting Labour, on the right hand side of the triptych.

So many dock leaves cannot soothe a nettled love
and so much spit can't break its enzymes down
a menstrual stain on childhood bedsheets
if she kept her dollshouse frame but sold the soul;
a car boot sale, a fiver
no tiny mismatched family could flourish there
no tiny chair would hold that weary Sylvanian.

Who profits from my wearing suncream in the dark?
I am sleep's priest defrocked
enrolling in a cycle-to-work scheme
then confronted with the mass weigh-in
on the bus a discarded newspaper out of sync with the
hawker in my pocket: a crisis of care,

a sick note culture, a laugh and a joke.

What if I'm not the woman I thought you were—
well, focus first on finding an NHS dentist
through the mirage
she is smiling but it doesn't reach her mouth
kitten licks are sandpaper still
I am eroding
but it is the only affection
in the queue—
thank you for your time.

Diptych

In ekphrastic stuckness,
pinned, Remedios Varo 'Rheumatic Pain I',
to architecture.

The load-bearing wall
of experience
keeping upright, even though

Crumble, wait—the communication of pain is beyond language
is what can't be spoken, and
finding in your adolescent middle-age that
everything is beyond language
so, better not to speak!
Cannot see pain, like weather, so
it simply happens

This too is articulation of power the
beyond-words the
articulate and there is a naming of things which cuts and ruins
and there is a naming of things without
stable category, the imposition of make-it-fit,
that Lispectorian specificity of many things nameable:

capitalism or
Elbit or
he who pressed the button or
she who took the shot or
they who profit directly or
we who profit indirectly or
a mood or
a whim or

a mission or
a decision or
a genocide or
'today' or

'I am in pain'

Suspended, Remedios Varo 'Rheumatic Pain II'
in view of the castle,
still—say it.

Royston Smith MP

Misery loves cornering you in the Sainsbury's up the road
to demand it, on-the-spot, real-time,
no lag no catch-up no secretary no 'no debate' no 'no casework'
no 'local lad made good worked in a bike shop has the
lowest attendance rate of any Member'
it would impress me if I weren't a potential investment zone
incapable of feeling just, absolutely gridded.

Cornering you in the Sainsbury's up the road is of course
absolutely fucking pointless but Misery has not
been able to see a GP
since Misery's second child was born and, it's worth a go—
that's the joke. For a fuller dissection of the set-up and execution,
do send me an email. I'll respond (that's the punchline)
within five working days. Do you get it?

The Sainsbury's up the road has two exits,
not ideal for cornering for conversation
or for Misery coming up from below to take it back:
Bitterne Road West reclaimed and dug-out, piles of concrete
obstructing the bike lanes—sorry. I can't do this, electoralism
mid-the-cereals, the least Romantic day of my whole 53 week
tax year this, uninspiring slop: mass produced.

Extrapolate

There is just so much metadata
a code-ghost with every *anything*

If I speak I am
a series of notes on a right-click

Do they know
I am checking?

Part III—Elegy

*

Impossible to cover everything wrong with this
then, impossible to deliver a holistic assessment:

and yet.

Outlet

We were on something that was ninety percent the something
we are used to but
ten percent something shimmering else
which made you hungry for explanation and
here I come:

The natural tuning of a brass instrument
is dependent on the length and width of the brass
which widens in circumference as it reaches towards the bell
though the point and rate at which it widens differs
which of course affects the tuning
you may recognise as the arpeggiated violence of a Remembrance
do doooooo
do doooooo
in Bb major and the higher the pitch the greater
the variation the flexibility
a scream of freedom finally no longer tied to the gaps
between pressure and silence
I get ahead of myself
from posthorn to trombone to trumpet
the length of brass is switched out
dependent on the valves, you press and you
cut things off you open things up
you make different kinds of space inside
you are free at a lower pitch to make something move between
first and fifth
your fingers, your lips,
I have a bad overbite and I would bleed
worse the higher I went, the closer to sound
set free from width and length

and then I was raped
and so I didn't go to music college.

Tuesday

Struggle bus
everything's a *brigade*.

Imagine haunting your own house
embarrassing.

>   *'Isn't it great they've invented a plastic speculum!*
>   *Single-use, disposable!'*

as if that was ever the fucking problem,
the reuse.

If you can get through the day without saying 'ouch'
you win.

Sorry I didn't like your buzzy debut *piece*,
read it in the bath when I was never out of it
and it ruined bathtime. Worse than the twitching
of my spinal muscle,
do you know how big an insult that is, for me to launch,
from here?

The cat lived to twenty-eight,
feels unfair for her to get that far,
only to stop. Should just let her keep going.

In Public

1.30 arrival, pulling in
an overwhelming noise
on the train before everyone's finished getting off
a broken social contract I have not finished getting off
a buzz scroll ancient endless
libidinal
papyrus leads out the sarcophagus into the world
and it's just not right behaviour cricket on
unboundaried without connection an eyeroll without target

sat in the waiting room where
we barely wait
we lucky few
we called-in
we England
pint and pleasant sickness
practically fucking numinous but
losing pallour—you told me this was an appointment
instead a sucked lollipop
cartoon care
almost beehive
it is a *waiting slot*

7.30 arrival I mine your experience
I have put you in this poem
but it happens always

5.30 arrival
six second noise
a telling off
a massacre

a remix
an undertone
a deepfake orgasm
a defection
a goal
a tutorial
a suicide
a slip

measure six times seventy six of this 1800 seconds
of potentially-your-name.

Return

'Get through Terminal 5 duty free without crying' challenge
I still expect it
I am spoilt, that way

Appeal to an imagined past
mythos in
retrograde
Ratatouille but it's a whole fucking country
and I'm a bowl of soup
take that hat off, you wanker

The simplicity of the statement,
we have brought this supposed sense
into the whole wide sky
I'm embarrassed for us
emergency button please you don't sell Pringles on this flight
because that's an *EasyJet thing*
you know, you said it, two rows behind
but I need to tell you, hold you in space suspended you can react here,
with me,
it's okay,
it's absolutely fucking hilarious—
you say nothing, this is your job,
of course.

Child Poem

I clutched a scrap:
at least I am on a bench, in the Winter sun, miserable
beyond belief—
I could be not
on a bench or, listen to the peppy swing! The cover band
is bopping in the breeze and yes this would be worse.
You are now, not
or soon to be, not

Said I would stop
writing about this now it's been nearly two years
but the form of address has shifted she is
now you there are five of you I can't contain
these voices to appropriate
but if I stop to sick you up or blow, frosty,
you'll die off completely

Like you already haven't, because I am so.
In my sleep, you have taken some pills and they won't work
right away,
so I have some time, again, and I am not
chased by a boulder down through the jungle,
towards the interface:
timed. Counting down, exactly.
It is shuddering, slow, exceedingly,
ice in the veins, miracle morning,
dreadful sleep. There is nothing else to say,
it just keeps happening, the not.

Today I got a twelve pence reduction in my council tax
which is lyrical, now. I could not express myself better than that.

Or if I could, it slipped away when you did
and you and you and you and you are now, slipping.
Taking the last scrap of my
emotion, intuitive kernel, welling. Selfish you.

Tired

Slip into can-do plucky attitude
my whip-smart
dog on a leash
cream on a cone
timely woman.
Open her mouth and
see? Shells.
My logician here tells me
it can be all worked out
like tension, accrued
I prefer the pushing to the
rolling back.
Quick review of the day shows me:
'magic moments
they're really out there
and oh—here comes another one'
three forty-two pee em.
Sense of the gravity of the recitation
resting, a lily-pad on my
pickled mind,
too-long tongue through the gaps and
tug it, take it with you,
I lap that shit up,
could come in useful. I only want
to lend myself to the cause
and you only want to pretend
you speak for me
but what an end to it all,
pass me the song of myself
if I can remember.

(*)

I am selfish:
I won't kill myself
because I don't want people to talk about my potential
or imagine an alternate present to here: I have children.

Words Mean Things?

Passes me another bottle of Coke,
the doctor, on his rounds in hopes of
internal fizz, bringing it up, whatever it is,
microplastic-charged. I am infused,
everything I cannot say, snapping photos,
happy birthday: here is the hospital.

> *Clamouring in bedsheets, oversensitive rub I*
> *dream of an etymological materialism,*
> *a student asks why there is so much French*
> *so I tell him, asyllabically.*

Meanwhile the theft of understanding
I am seething with jealousy, there goes
someone with normal feet
wearing my unbroken shoes.

> *It is quantum complex to win a physical examination*
> *on the application lottery,*
> *the clapping slower and slower each Wednesday*
> *to become a single meeting of the palms—and what is that?*

Slice yourself open and scrabble
for purchase, for nine pounds and sixty-five pence
you have made it to the pharmacy spine
so cling on, fucker.

> *Back at the hospital I am a secret in 'SURGERY'*
> *front-facing zoom down the throat,*
> *make it so: we cannot understand each other*
> *because you are rushed off your feet*

and I choked on a bit of kebab last night.

It's fine because it's funny.

More Of That

Slip-up, girl
virtuoso, with
virtue, but
wonky, so
dog-ear, the
racial history of the pill intersecting
history of depression down the line so
doctor-patient confidentiality
fucked me
four aunts, homicidal tendencies
let the dam drop like bad post,
coupons unsolicited,
sobbing on the dockside,
it was a rush—that I can say for sure,
and little else.

When the environment is overlaid with a filter called 'cooption'
ready to make its way into my mouth like flying ant day
is that passivity or activity, it certainly tastes active,
you have to be very careful not to say
This Might Be Bad, Somehow,
lest too many of them fly down your throat up it comes the acid
a great burping mess: Ban Contraception.

Why? Well, bloodied pad on the old school wall
slapped in complicated grief thoughts
about the conkers, how they triggered something in me
on that side and the other:
retread, step again, but this time left foot.

Filling out the PIP forms is an exercise in

weeding out the ones who cannot twist language
to their needs,
so fuck you if you can't lie-but-not-lie-or-something-like-it:
go back to work, where all the honesty is.

Soon, ladies, we'll be
having surgery in one of those shops
selling alcoholism and sentiment:
Live, Laugh, Liver.

Showing your passport before you give birth
like every single membrane is reconceptualised as a border
and you are to be crossed
from the unborn to the breathing, burden on the state
like speaking, sound makes its way behind and beyond
so do you have the relevant paperwork?
Were you given permission?
Are those tears eking their way out of you?
Are you letting the dog out?
Were you given permission?
Can I come in?
I'm coming in.

Repatriation

In the hotel in Egypt not that hotel not that room
how did she do it what did she use
these ceilings are too high but were those ones—
hope it was a cable not a dressing gown belt

Would be able to see the hotel room in that video she recorded
never watch let it be
so every hotel room is that one

There is a great big nothing where it was,
such that it does and does not overpower what it is:
mystery and tidbit encourage each other,

All hours now of the star and we are all vulture,
picking at scraps of the moment we could not witness
so the most nourishing thing left is the method

I know you feel this too—
the cliff the symbol the image the burn of it—
can't touch your throat

> *We were told "you do not want to see her body."*
> *but someone saw it and in the period of time*
> *where we had reported her missing to Interpol and were screaming*
> *at the hotel staff to open the door,*
> *somebody already had*
> *claim to the image.*

Silence imposed by fear of appropriation
compounded by those others
say first that and now—

Meanwhile, the Queen died
at the Windsor Palace Hotel, Alexandria,
not a mention of it, on the roof

Return to Gatwick, a memorial poster
we pretend is for her,
whisper to the box, in its stapled shroud.

Lining

The thing is I have filled it in before
The thing is we are all of us stardust
The thing is this handful of stardust is a gynaecologist
The thing is he is my twelfth
is they have all been different
is believing
is inside me
is a great nothing.

> *Two paracetamol taken the morning of*
> *that great nothing needed to be sucked out swift*
> *I found, wordless, no exposition:*
> *tiny knife and silence.*

Sat stock still in Nando's staring into a paper bag:
two fish in plastic, in water in plastic,
remember someone else's tiny something and
they couldn't get it out, it said—no,
they think she will be stuck with it, out of juice
simply sitting and I suppose
that metal doesn't take and take like
flesh-potential-flesh and doesn't replicate it only
remains, coin-stuff, spread-wings.

> *Back again back further back to*
> *number eleven with the glasses and the pen*
> *chewing my words my girl-question*
> *took me so much to ask it took me pains*
> *to say 'how long, before I—'*
> *looking him in the eye with a wry wryness*
> *'Six weeks, mate. Sorry'.*

> *Didn't even look me in the eye but*
> *perhaps I would've preferred him peering around,*
> *somewhat concerned,*
> *for someone.*

It will grow back and I will feel it
is that not individual talent I have made a
glistening error, and I am tipped slowly forwards again
to catch a swinging doctor-door and two kind
reapers in white say:
it is over and you will be back
like a sunset or an argument.

State Care

'Not properly refrigerated'
hanged decomposed cremated boxed
'is that a bomb' at the border
language a hard, cruel barrier

'cause of death: unknown'
a death at your own hand
not recognised, somehow more honest
in its quantum mystery.

Ad Asteracaeae

Shut in the cupboard with the CBT homework
half-done I whisper Michael I found the lettuce funny
caught myself up in a snarl of theoretical string and
limbs through the tangle I flail, onto your desk
I'll get back to work when I figure it out:
how to avoid subsumption, when all those
newspapers become wrappings down the chippy,
the ink bleeds and we digest it, fish and the British
media's recuse to meaning—it is absurd and I must recognise it
but the way she wilted was a state-sanctioned giggle
while the market swept.

Temptation to reduce or render shock-sex to avoid
salient critique:
great tongue on the cunt of capital. Derivatives,
squirting and piss-not-piss.
That'll do it, accidental.

When you're sanctioned for the first time it feels
like vernacular exostosis,
mute shake of the head,
breaking every shoe, bursting through leather-like-money
burned and tossed and pornographic:
Why aren't you more careful?
They're only bones.

Retroverted uterus wedged between
the sacrum and the bladder, perpendicular to the placement
of the normal uterus
Retroflexed position, curled up like a prawn
Anteverted or in hyperanteflexion.

One could measure one's cardiovascular health
in how much time they have spent consistently
running down fascists in the streets
which is another reason why one might become a hunt saboteur
but one, two, three discs out of place there is glory in admin
when you know who'll be doing the running.
I would move you around like a limited homebrew campaign
if you'd let me in, love.

Smear

Complex history of excavation
said she grew up wanting to be an 'Egyptologist'
asking me what I do for a living as she
opens me up,
how many of the objects in the room are Cobalt-tinged
how much of this place riven at the surface
just a scooping, panning, sifting—
unconscionable music to distract me,
what calms me down is nothing,
what keeps me still is somewhere else,
wriggle through the imaging
to frustrate the process
delay my own capture, glowing instant—
it helps nobody.

Unaccounted For In The Studies

Bit of fluff in the bath,
attempt at capture with thumb and forefinger,
endless orgasmic frustration,
they called it *plateau*,
I call it somatic OCD, perverse,
it ruptures pleasure, confuses things,
like kink but badder—
can't play my fucking colouring-in game on my phone
it all gets too much for me,
too close.

Listen to your body all well and good
I didn't sleep last night because I could hear my knees,
making visitation with my upper arms and
there I was, puppeted, and there's no cutting those strings—
it is a cringing shame
that pang on seeing *imperfect teeth*.

Your blog currently also has one introductory post
(and I've lost it, did you delete it or is this a failure of SEO?
Google is useless now, and you are no advert for the desirable,
promotion and sponsorship)
heart emoji react in excelsis deo.

Make a list of everything wrong with me and call it a poem,
would be preferable for whoever mans the e-consults,
but is it *critique*, just to *tell you*? My back screams,
I put the book down,
I remain,
I think it is.

When the bell used to toll three-quarters
I felt stomach-sucked from time
that town crier ditty
Omelas is in the volta—the lack of imagination
I confess I struggle.

A summer cold,
lots of them still about,
like gangs of teenage girls on corner-shop corners,
long shadows longer at 7.03 today,
endless lug of it.

*

Took her three years to get diagnosed
oh such a *patient*
woman.

I Am Well

Citronella candle
moth to a dog-whistling flame

back to trepanation
she did it neatly on the live,
utterly gougeless,
I saw the spirits leave—
shocked react

a life worth living
is any life
but what's knowing that worth
at the end of the day:
the night.

Track my shipping
I am in transit yet,
but when I am out for delivery
you will want to know.

Dead Skin

Hack at it
when you slipstream past on your way to
work in the other room or the other one
like, fork pricks on sausages
so you burn but you don't peel.
It is a sunny day
of sirens sucking at the juncture where
now meets yesterday, flame on Fairy Liquid palms.
The only way out is
through the cubicle dividers like a giant toddler kicking
it was so silly of us to start respecting our toys
too late realising they weren't ours at all
then again—no, actually they are, give them back
to everyone.
It's funny because
when I found out about dust I sat still
for ten straight days without moving to try and trick them:
my house, and my body, and the air. Give it back,
stay still, don't drift or swallow.
I take up my arms again
stretch, six AM, shoulder it: everything.
When I am nothing but a cartoon shape of myself
carved through the wall and gone
then I'll really know what it's like.

Two Factor

One day they will tell her
she must download an app to get in touch
with her daughter.

I will be informed of this via
carelessly worded spelling mistake mailing list inbox blight
'Dearest Katherine,'
straight to spam.

We will never speak again—
they have made it too difficult
and besides I can't authenticate shit
from up here, in the secret dreamworld space,
where I am stored I am
sorry, Mum.

I did not keep a diary for you
for I did not think you would die,
and you haven't, it is only that you cannot catch the bus
because the bus is in your brain and
your brain is a computer and
you cannot use it and
you are out of touch and
you are not trying hard enough and
you are entitled to an extra three pounds a month and
you did not claim it fast enough and
you have missed your chance and
we are trying to make things more accessible for you and
we are invested in your welfare and
we are working on it and
we will be rolling out new online services very soon and

we would very much appreciate it and
we will be in touch and

The myelin sheath is an insulating layer
formed around the nerves
which is scarred beyond repair.
What are you going to do about it?
Cells shaking in the wind like a naked whippet.

Kitchen Table

Origin of the family is the
family is the family is the family is the family is the
family, each unhappy alike in
born astride a grave of dignity
up from which the preverbal scream
demands an answer: translate *girlhood*
as if it exists, then write your piece,
no need even for the side-by-side
they'll simply know.

When all I can think to polish, sand is
'just cleaning up in here'
I have put it in poems before
but to lie there screaming
confronted with the complex history of the vacuum cleaner
hissing whose labour is saved and
how do the standards adapt
I am bloodied and burnt
wishing it was only dust to suck.

Sorry

Seems like everyone has endo these days
or they're all ADHD or left-handed or possessed
but I can't make everyone soup enough
with two big pans and, like, gumption

Sit down next to me and I can press my thigh
comfortingly against yours like nudge nudge
we are discovered and named and constructed
move away if you'd rather I didn't tonight

We have to let children learn these things
on their own:
comorbidities, interactions—
his old opioids, never returned to sender so it's
Serotonin-sickness-by-the-sea
locked in the train toilet, laughing and throwing up—
now that's a Roman retelling
lift me from the armpit and feed me grapes

I fake a new symptom every so often
to force an MRI
before it's too late.

Airing Cupboard

Hide and seek
the kind of place where you really don't want to be found
this is less a game, even less a test,
just don't come looking
I am on top of the wardrobe
I am in a secret sunbeam
I am inside myself, fingers curled
into the carpet,
I will come down after dinner
once you've all given up and I am trapped again
in the space between
resentment and relief,
where I am most at home. This is childhood,
bring me back there,
don't find me and don't let me leave.

Used to think there was a room behind the boiler
but never checked, because I knew there wasn't
even as I knew, for sure, there was,
and still is. I'm sorry, I am a giant now
I cannot fit behind, I cannot check
and so it is there. So something remains
that I can never see. This, and only this—
I inhale, silent sob.

Particulier

James told me he wanted to write a Universal poem
I want to write a poem about how I cannot stand to be touched
lightly
only with firm hand-span sinking
on both sides
this should be Universal.

> *He broke the mould when he made you*
> *such that you spilled out, jellying wriggle*
> *incapable of form,*
> *this is a poem about everything:*
> *Wittigian autism, rendered particular.*

Coming out to Mum for the second time in the car
after a psychiatrist told her the contents of my stomach—
this happens, clap and count the seconds: strike,
no crash, the weeping swaddles the weather.

> *Could always public sex, civil war,*
> *Old Basing slips around us, nettle-stung*
> *once again clench and imagine:*
> *si j'étais, si j'étais.*

Instead: over the hump and into the over-25s X Factor category
before you know it, plotted
on the actuarial graph of the cosmos
still: most of us are dead.

> *Taking stock of surroundings*
> *like the Millennium Dome, hollowed out, and*
> *somebody of marriageable age is*

> *simmering down to hiss in my ear:*
> *is writing about gay men a fetish?*
> *'Baby, all writing is fetish.'*

Language is cold here in the everyone
but we sit in it, bundling up against generality
and we talk about death – how could we not?
But we talk about fungus, too.

Dissolve

Healthcare
providing
comparison
for the rest of your life a
singular mothering
it lasted this long it hurt this much
I had this many stitches
I nearly died more than you did

who can blame this
come-out-on-top-need at the table
at the party
at the least appropriate moment—
discharge it

it would embarrassing to wake up
with umbilical cord
wrapped to trachea:
it's not exactly saying anything new, is it?

Instead: born asleep and shook,
a good vintage, undead.

Pathologic Hypertrophy

Could have chosen differently
double-bound on the teenage bed
please don't look
this is an introduction to the lie:
it is a private moment.

Option A will take the rest of your life
Option B will take the rest of your life
you will need parental permission for
one and not the other,
pull the curtain yank the chain.

In midst of double-sense,
a flowering rupture, a run from the scene
ripping things out
where you can: the spine and not the self,
it would be simpler.

Part IV—Reverie

Later

Writing less about triangulation now
there is no mode of speaking inherently *more*
this denial of 'better' no nihilistic resignation
it is communism, a world of it.

Locating precisely in the middle-that-is-not-half
a mathematics of speech-wank
a diacritic bore
there are good ways of growing sans diktat.

What aches, this world of mass disablement,
to be in it unmoving, lactic build-up of
there are just no words—
there never will be. So find new ways of speaking.

Resignation From

'What's cheapest way to stay warm?'
To eradicate cheapness
file off that hangnail on the final finger
pointing at the sun—this way!

Try that, lyric comes out, screed
in *sentences* no less, drink chalk bits
think, sipping from a trick held hand
my neural pathways sing:

This is that far-off thing, that unpaid undebt,
why—what day is it? It's Wednesday! and
no work to do, slippage is finally
a coarse wooly hug, the promise of a bounce.

Accidents like tiny griefs: to say
goodnight not goodbye
you too happy birthday, miss-mum—
good grief, it is no mistake to lack, see:

Hermit crabs lining up in order of size
pass along, house to smaller house, claw to little claw
we will clack and shuffle, someday soon
we will shuffle and clack.

Notes

'Resignation From', 'Ad Asteraceae' and 'Dead Skin' included in *Chicago Review* 2024

'loveless lexicon'—Cat Chong in conversation with Jen Hadfield for Guillemot Press, 'Inhabiting A Space of Love' (2020)

Epigraph: Umberto Eco from *The Name of the Rose* (1980)

Epigraph: Jacques Derrida from interview in *Diacritics* 2.4 (1972)

Further Derrida quotes throughout the book, from the same interview.

Epigraph: Cat Chong from *Dear Lettera 32* (2024)